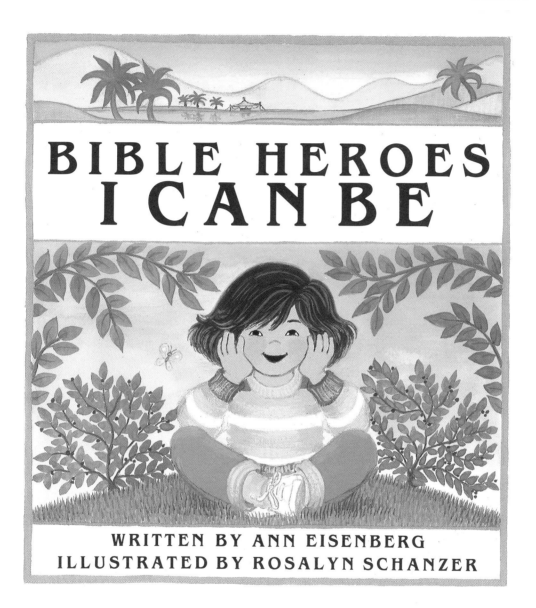

BIBLE HEROES
I CAN BE

WRITTEN BY ANN EISENBERG
ILLUSTRATED BY ROSALYN SCHANZER

KAR-BEN COPIES, INC.
ROCKVILLE, MD

To my parents
Sadie and Max
with love.
–A.E.

Library of Congress Cataloging-in-Publication Data

Eisenberg, Ann.
  Bible heroes I can be / Ann Eisenberg, illustrated by Roz Schanzer.
    p.   cm.
  Summary: Introduces such Biblical figures as Noah, Rebecca, and King David and
shows how their accomplishment and attributes can be emulated in modern life.
    ISBN 0-929371-09-7 — ISBN 0-929371-10-0 (pbk.)
    1. Heroes in the Bible—Juvenile literature. 2. Bible. O.T.—Juvenile literature. [1. Bible.
O.T.] I. Schanzer, Rosalyn, ill. II. Title.
BS551.2.E387   1990
220.9.2—dc20   89-48188
                                                                                          CIP
                                                                                          AC

BIBLE HEROES
I CAN BE

Noah built an ark.

I can build
lots of things.

Abraham and Sara
welcomed guests.

I like visitors, too.

Rebecca was kind
to animals.

So am I.

Joseph had
a colorful coat.

Just like mine.

Miriam watched over
her baby brother Moses.

I watch our baby, too.

Moses was
a good leader.

I am, too.

Joshua made
the walls fall down.

Oops, here they go!

Ruth gathered
food for Naomi.

I pick tomatoes
in our garden.

King David played
beautiful music.

So can I.

King Solomon
was very wise.

I learn
new things
every day.